Koalas

One of Australia's best-known ambassadors, the koala is frequently misnamed the koala bear. The koala is not in fact a bear but a marsupial, and is the only living species of its type. Almost exclusively a tree-living animal, it feeds on the leaves of only a few species of smooth-barked eucalypts.

Sharp claws, long arms and strong hands, which are able to grip branches firmly, enable the koala to climb smooth tree trunks. Usually as inoffensive as it looks, when frightened or angered, a koala uses its sharp claws effectively.

The koala carries its young in a pouch for five or six months and then on her back. When about eight months old, the cub is able to care for itself.

Kangaroos

Kangaroos are famous for carrying their young in a pouch. The newly-born kangaroo is tiny, about the size of a bean, and with uncanny instinct, it crawls through the mother's fur and enters the pouch, where it attaches itself to a teat. The 'joey' starts to leave the pouch at six months of age and finally vacates it seven or so weeks later.

The largest of the species is the giant red kangaroo, which favors the semi-arid plains of inland Australia, and the great grey kangaroo, whose preference is for forested country in coastal regions.

The long and heavy tail serves as a balance when the kangaroo is bounding at great speeds, and as a third leg when standing or moving slowly.

Wallabies

There is no distinct difference between kangaroos and wallabies other than size. Wallabies are smaller and they tend to inhabit more densely vegetated country than the kangaroos. The swamp wallaby *(above)* inhabits the moist gullies and thickets along the east coast of Australia. One of the more colorful members of the wallaby group is the rock wallaby *(left)*. Its feet have soft granular pads to prevent slipping and hence it moves around rocky outcrops with incredible agility and certainty.

opposite: One of the two surviving egg-laying mammals, the platypus is difficult to keep in captivity. These photographs were taken at the wildlife sanctuary at Healesville, Victoria, where the platypus has been bred successfully. In the water, its webbed front feet act as broad paddles, while the hind feet trail behind and together with the tail, give stability and directional control. In its natural environment, the platypus nests in burrows on river banks, moving around mainly at dusk or early morning to feed on crayfish, tadpoles and other insects that it shovels from the river bottom with its broad bill.

Echidnas

Commonly known as the spiny ant-eater, the echidna is Australia's other surviving egg-laying mammal. As its common name suggests, the echidna feeds mainly on ants and termites, which it licks up with its long sticky tongue. If disturbed, the echidna's instinctive reaction is to burrow straight downwards and once half-buried, it is almost impossible to dislodge.

opposite: The wombat has a reputation for being a powerful digger, with a big appetite for the roots of shrubs and trees. Its stocky build and shovel-like claws enable it to excavate its burrow, sometimes roomy enough for a child to enter.

Parrots

left: The delicately colored turquoise parrot inhabits the north-western tablelands of New South Wales. Once considered to be in danger of becoming extinct, these parrots were bred successfully in captivity and have become re-established in their former haunts.

above: The beautiful rose and grey colors of the galah provide a spectacular sight when a flock of these birds is in flight. Being given to much chatter and hence its popularity as a cage-bird, the galah has carved a niche for itself in Australian speech with the colorful simile, 'mad as a gumtree full of galahs'.

right: Red, blue and yellow flash in the plumage of the rainbow lorikeet. Belonging to the honey-parrot group, so-called because of their nectar diet, the lorikeet unfortunately does not confine itself to nectar and frequently attacks fruit in orchards.

Parrots

The rosella *(above)* was first observed near Rosehill, a district near Sydney, and hence was originally called a rosehiller. In the early days of settlement, it was a popular bird for puddings and pies, as well as sending alive to England.

The lorikeets *(above right)* were photographed at the Currumbin sanctuary on the Gold Coast, Queensland. The sanctuary is famous for its wild lorikeets, which are fed twice daily. Hundreds of these brightly colored parrots fly down from the bushland to feed on plates of bread and honey.

The strong beak of the white cockatoo *(right)* is frequently used to strip bark from trees and to break into the wood in search of grubs. A flock of these parrots can cause considerable damage to wheat and kindred crops. Wary and intelligent, white cockatoos when raiding a wheat field post sentinels around the borders of the crop, to keep a lookout for any sign of danger.

above: The crimson and blue of the rosella is its mature plumage; the young rosella is a green bird. This broad-tailed parrot is very familiar to Australians; its gaily colored portrait is the well-known brand of a large manufacturing company.

left: Inhabiting the inland areas of Australia, the corella is known as a reliable 'water guide', for it is seldom found far from permanent water. It feeds on bulbous roots, which it excavates with its powerful beak. As a talker, the corella is one of the most vocal of Australia's birds.

Kookas

An outburst of harsh and hearty laughter, the 'song' of the kookaburra, is a familiar sound in Australia. The kookaburra is the largest member of the kingfisher family, but unlike its kin, it rarely fishes. Its reputation as a snake-killer may not be deserved, although small snakes, rats and young birds are part of its diet.

Not all kookaburras have a hearty laugh. The blue-winged kookaburra laughs after a fashion, but it lacks the volume and heartiness of the laughing kookaburra. The young of the laughing kookaburra utter croaking sounds until, encouraged if not actually taught by the older birds, they are able to produce the true laughing call.

Emus

Women's liberation is not an issue for the female emu, for she has been liberated for a long time. It is the male bird who makes the nest, incubates the large green eggs and becomes the guardian of the young chicks. The emu, Australia's largest bird, is unable to fly, but has a vestigial wing held close to the body. An emu, together with a kangaroo, supports Australia's coat-of-arms.

right: The female lyrebird lacks the liberation of the female emu and is sentenced to four months of solitary work, building the home, brooding the egg and rearing the chick. Meanwhile, her male partner sings and displays, strutting on his mound with the famous tail fanned in a gossamer-like arch. The tail feathers vibrate as this wonderful mimic goes through his repertoire.

Possums

Possums have made certain adaptations for their arboreal way of life. They are able to grip branches firmly, assisted by their feet, which can grip like human hands, strong claws and either a long thin tail, which curls around the branch or a bushy tail, which serves as a balance. The common grey brush-tailed possum continues to prove its adaptability to a changing environment by frequently taking up residence in the roofs of houses rather than trees. One of the more interesting types of possum is the glider possum *(right)*, aptly named, for when it leaps from bough to bough, it is supported by narrow flying membranes along the sides of its body.

opposite: Although the dingo is closely related to the domesticated dog, it has some distinctive features. Its ears remain permanently erect and it yelps and howls rather than barks. The dingo is a very cunning hunter and a menace to livestock. In an attempt to control their numbers, there is a bounty on dingo scalps. Compared with Australia's 'living fossils', the platypus and the echidna, the dingo is a relative newcomer, possibly being introduced by the Aborigines or other wandering native people from the north.

Dingo

Penguins

Penguins, looking like little gentlemen in dress suits, coming ashore at Phillip Island, Victoria, to feed their young after a day's fishing. Though clumsy as they waddle or shuffle on land, penguins are graceful and speedy in water, being the champion divers of the feathered world. Unlike most water birds, penguins use their wings as propellors rather than their webbed feet, when swimming.

right: The black swan was received with some wonder when first seen by Dutch sailors, familiar only with the white plumaged kind, while exploring the river estuaries on the west coast of Australia at the end of the seventeenth century. Many pairs of swans form a breeding colony, making large, open, thick-walled nests in a swamp area or shallow lagoon, areas also frequented by cormorants, seen in the foreground of this photograph.

Seals

Of all the marine mammals that inhabit the oceans around the Australian coastline, the seal is the one that emerges from the sea to spend a significant time on Australian shores. The white-necked hair seals, pictured on this page, bear on their necks and shoulders a mane of coarse almost white hair, which, luckily for them, is almost valueless to the furrier.

right: During springtime, glorious massed displays of wattle blossom can be seen throughout the country, in the bushland and in city gardens, varying in size from small shrubs to large trees. It was an environmental accident that gave Australia the name wattle to describe the type of plants known as acacias. Early settlers required protection against the weather and built shelters in the English 'wattle-and-daub' style — twigs plastered with mud. The twigs came from the acacia trees and thus these trees became known in Australia as wattles.

Wildflowers

left: The brilliant red of the Sturt desert pea transforms the sandy plains of the semi-arid inland after good rains in spring. A trailing plant, its clusters of scarlet blooms hang vertically and its leaves are covered with silky hairs that give the plant a grey-green appearance.

left below: The large bottle-brush flower heads of the banksia, a tree named after Sir Joseph Banks, the naturalist who accompanied Captain Cook. Its saw-toothed leaves, extraordinary range of flower colors and oddly shaped fruits combine to make the banksia an unusual species of Australian flora.

below: One of Australia's most arrestingly beautiful flowers, the waratah grows in sandy soils, largely in northern New South Wales, and flowers from September to November.